Spark your creativity on the go!

Take this portable drawing pad with you anywhere to exercise your mind and activate your imagination. At first glance, the squiggles and shapes may look like abstract objects. But look a little closer, or flip them around—do you see something else? See a cactus? Add some thorns and place it in a desert. Or maybe you see a person? Doodle some arms and legs and a sweet outfit. A skyscraper? Give it some windows and surround it with a city.

There are no rules, no wrong answers, and no drawing skills required!

Doodling is a great way to open up the creative corners of your brain. Use this pad while trave... waiting ... Soon y ... dreamt ... Theory ...

Share your doodles and see what others are drawing:

#doodletheory

dletheoryclub

odletheory.club

M000072946

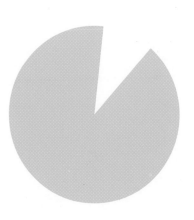

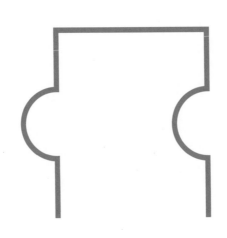

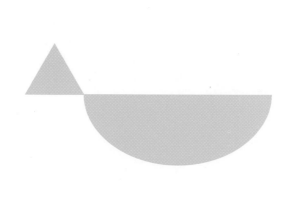

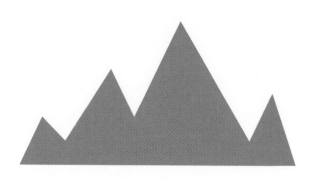

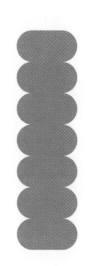

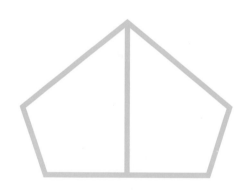

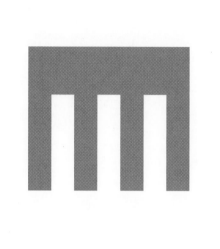

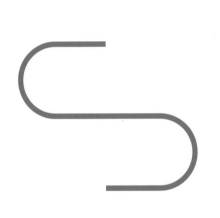

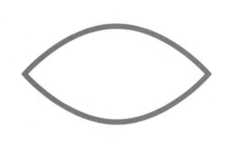

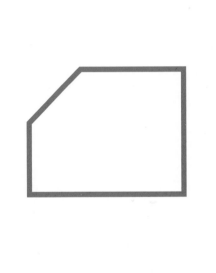

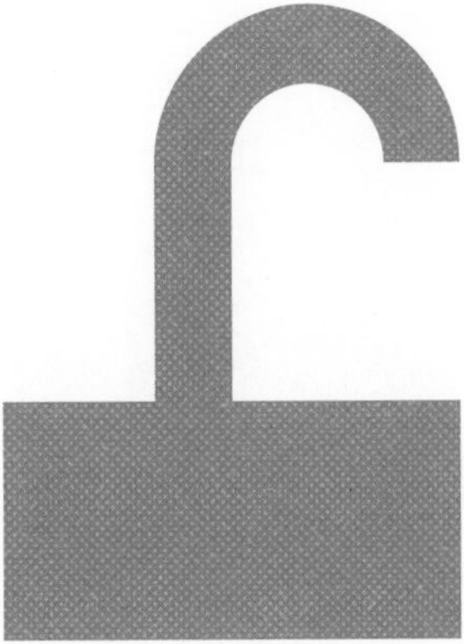

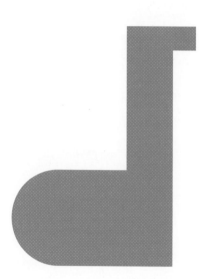

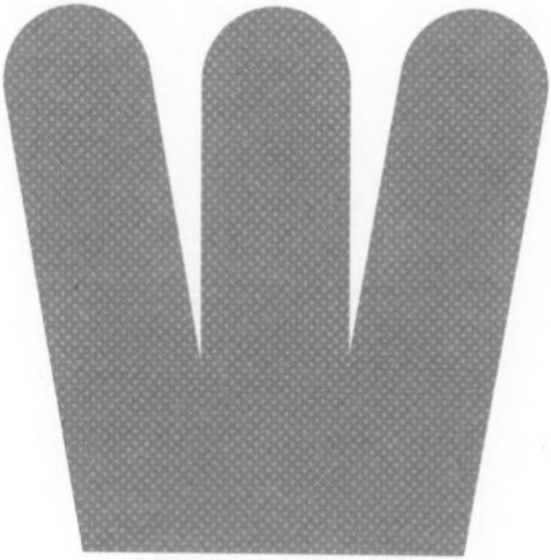

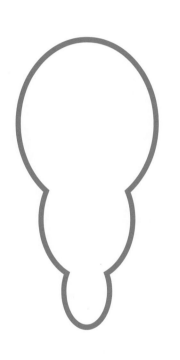

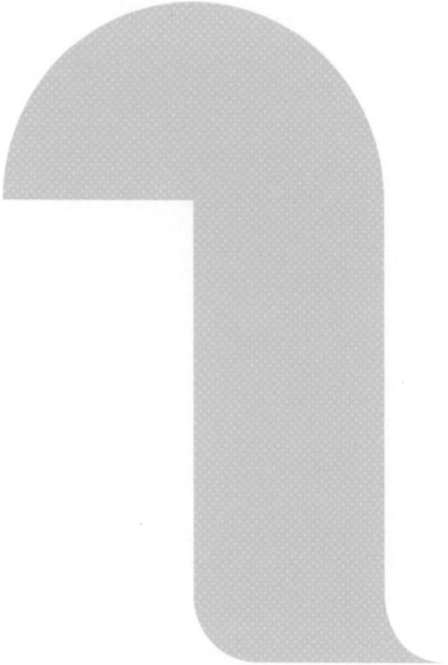

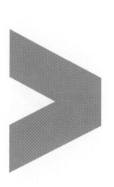

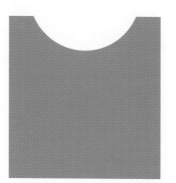

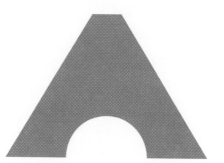

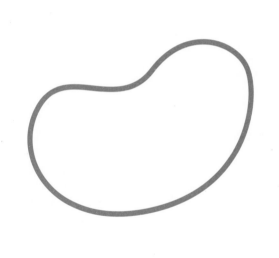

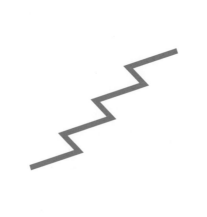

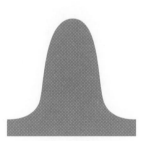

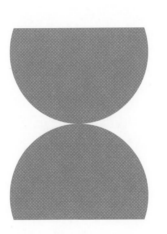

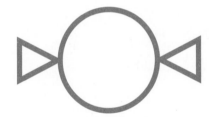

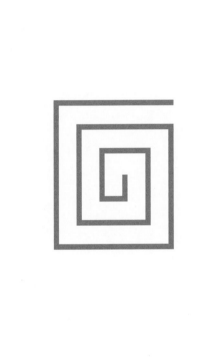

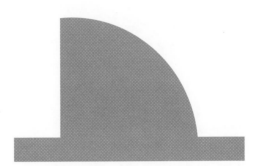

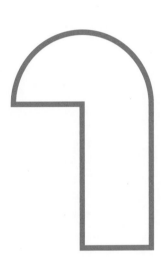

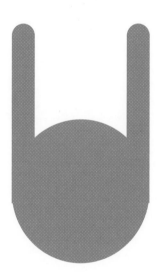

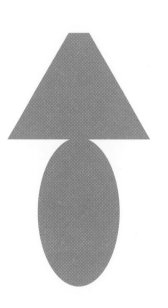

ISBN: 978-1-4521-5123-6

Manufactured in China

www.doodletheory.club

Also available: *Doodle Theory: Create Amazing
Doodles with Hundreds of Starter Squiggles*

10 9 8 7 6 5 4 3 2 1

Chronicle Books
680 Second Street
San Francisco, CA 94107
www.chroniclebooks.com